New England

a fresh perspective

PHOTOGRAPHY AND NARRATIVE BY

Alan Murtagh

STOCK STILLS PHOTOGRAPHY • GLOUCESTER, MASSACHUSETTS

NEW ENGLAND | *a fresh perspective*

PHOTOGRAPHY AND NARRATIVE BY
Alan Murtagh

BOOK DESIGN
Nancy Starkman
StarPrintBrokers.com

ISBN: 978-0-9889749-0-6

PRINTED IN SOUTH KOREA

Introduction

When I set out to gather material for this book, I included amongst my equipment the latest in GPS-based mobile navigation devices.

Unfortunately, such devices are not of such great value in New England.

Although the distances appeared small, (compared to anywhere else in North America) the travel time indicated turned out to be only an approximation, for nearly every trip revealed totally unexpected awe-inspiring scenic vistas; fascinating historical monuments; unique museums; picturesque villages and restaurants catering to every possible food preference.

Add to these pleasant distractions the sheer diversity of New England, which is not only about the changes of the four seasons and the widely varying and fast changing weather, but also the contrasts for all the senses—the architectural delights of historical buildings and modern structures in the cities; the different character of Industrial Revolution-era riverside mill towns and the picturesque coastal towns, the summer beaches and winter ski slopes; the modern, bustling progressive cities and the quiet, lost-in-time villages; the raucous noises of a Red Sox game at Fenway, the harmony of a Tanglewood concert, the thunder of the Atlantic surf and the haunting call of the loons on a Maine lake, all of which combine to make an interesting adventure possible every single day.

Although every picture supposedly tells a story, it was not until I researched the unique and fascinating histories of these images that I discovered a new dimension to add to what was already an interesting photograph.

In this book you will learn of:

- A 200-million-year-old natural phenomenon—discovered only 200 years ago by a 93-year old woman, who was fishing in a mountain river.

- An Army Engineer, survivor of many battles of the Civil War, who designed a metal lighthouse, and then built it inside the older structure it was to replace.

- A world-famous scenic railway—constructed only because the inventor became disoriented on the mountain and decided that there had to be a better way down.

Whether you have a passion for outdoor recreation, an interest in the arts, a curiosity for history, or prefer hunting for antiques or browsing boutiques, the six states that make up New England will more than satisfy your needs.

Just remember to allow extra time.

I would like to dedicate this book to my wife Peg, for without her insight, encouragement and patience, this book would probably still have been finished—it certainly would not have been as good.

—ALAN MURTAGH

CONNECTICUT

Connecticut River, near Old Lyme

A Whale by the Tail

Although this looks like a very relaxed moment for the trainer and Juno, a 10-year-old male beluga whale, this is actually part of an important training session. The Mystic Aquarium's belugas are trained to display their flukes (tails) so that they can voluntarily participate in their own health care. Blood draws, for example, can be taken from the flukes. The whales would not normally display their flukes this way.

Seeking a Seal of Approval?

Sea lions have fine motor control of their nostrils. This California sea lion appears to be demonstrating her bubble-blowing prowess as she slowly descends before an observant animal care intern. Known as New England's hands-on aquarium, Mystic Aquarium offers animal encounters, interactive experiences and dynamic learning opportunities.

Beauty and the Beast

(right)

*I*n the background, the 170 foot Schooner *Mystic,* built in 2007 to be used as a charter vessel. She can carry 34 passengers in comfortable cabins on long cruises.

In the foreground, a classic tugboat. Built in Camden, Maine in 1954, she is 37 feet long and has been converted into a private boat.

The Sailor's Classroom

(below, right)

*A*s the Danish vessel *Georg Stage,* the 111-foot schooner *Joseph Conrad* trained over 4,000 cadets. In 1936, crewed by mostly boys, she completed a 58,000 mile circumnavigation. Transferred to The Mystic Seaport in 1947, the ship is now an exhibit; and a training ship for the Mystic Mariner Program and the Museum's educational programs.

Long Greens and Oysters

(below)

*M*ilford is proud of 2 things—the second longest town green in New England; and the annual Oyster Festival, held on the third Saturday of August. Drawing over 50,000 attendees, "Oysterfest" is billed as the largest one-day festival in the New England region and is listed amongst the top 10 annual events in Connecticut.

The Inn of Dark Shadows

Although The Griswold Inn, located in Essex, Connecticut, is significant as the oldest continuously-run tavern in the US; it is probably just as well known as the "Collinsport Inn," the setting for the original 1960's vampire soap opera—"Dark Shadows."

Architectural Student's Delight

(top and below, right)

The diverse mix of architectural styles seen in Yale's buildings, towers, lawns, courtyards, walkways, gates and arches led one architecture critic to describe it as *"the most beautiful urban campus in America."*

City in the Clouds

(below, left)

Architect James Gamble Rogers said of the Sterling Memorial Library that it was— *"as near to modern Gothic as we dared to make it."*

The mysterious disposition of surplus building materials has resulted in myths and legends on the Yale campus. Some claim that a small castle, and even a complete miniature city, are built on the roof.

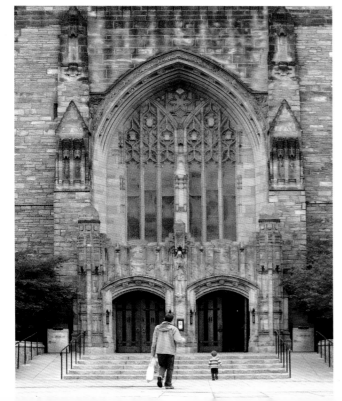

9

An Adventurer and a Hero Lived Here

In 1820, Nathaniel Brown Palmer, captain of the 47-foot sloop *Hero,* discovered Palmer Land, a peninsula in Antarctica.

In 1840, his brother, Alexander Smith Palmer, was presented with a gold medal by Queen Victoria for rescuing the crew of the shipwrecked *Eugenie.*

This 16-room Victorian mansion was built by the two brothers in 1852.

Potted Perennial Pick Up

This display at the Roseledge Inn's Farm Store features a line-up of white and red 14-inch potted geraniums; the bed of the truck has trays of 4-inch herbs; hanging in the door of the cab is a scarlet red ivy geranium and the front of the truck has a display of potted perennials.

George Washington Danced Here

The Peck Tavern House, on US 1 in Old Lyme, CT, was built in 1680. Opened as a tavern in 1769 by owner John Peck, it served coach travelers on the Boston Post Road.

In 1776, guest George Washington danced in the town's ballroom, which was located on the second floor of this house.

A Meeting of the Preston Chicken Association

Amongst the perennial gardens of the homestead formerly owned by John Meech, now the Roseledge Country Inn, these chickens seem to be gathered to discuss whatever chickens discuss, while a rooster stands guard. The Roseledge Bed and Breakfast Inn offers country lodging and accommodations in Preston, CT.

All Aboard For an Adventure

The most popular and well-known attraction in Essex, CT, is the Essex Steam Train & Riverboat ride. The 50-mile train ride takes passengers from Essex to Deep River, where they may board the riverboat *Becky Thatcher,* for a trip up the Connecticut River, then back to the train.

A Well-Traveled Veteran

Built by the American Locomotive Company of Dunkirk, NY in 1920, Steam Engine No. 40 had a long and interesting career prior to pulling the Essex Steam Train. She hauled timber in Oregon, and freight and passenger trains in North Carolina. The engine is one of less than 200 operable steam locomotives in the US.

A Long Walk to Lunch

The distinctive tower of the Aetna Building in Hartford tops the largest colonial revival-style building in the world. Four and one-half million locally made bricks were used on the exterior of the building. The corridor on the 'A' floor, which runs from the Sigourney Street lobby to the cafeteria, is 1/8th of a mile long.

An Early Flasher With Nasty Noises

The New London Harbor Light, built in 1801, was one of the earliest American lighthouses with a flashing light, which helped distinguish it from nearby houses.

In 1904 a fog horn was installed. However, it made a sound so objectionable that a petition for it's removal included the signature of the Mayor of New London.

Retired Lighthouse. With Carousel.

Although only functional as an aid to navigation for 73 years, the New Haven Light House forms the centerpiece of Lighthouse Point Park in New Haven.

This adjacent building houses a fully functional, 1916 vintage carousel. A novel "Adopt-A-Horse" program was developed to help pay for the restoration of most of the 72 horses.

Where The Twain Did Meet

One hopes that when Samuel Langhorne Clemens (a.k.a. Mark Twain) said—*"it is less trouble and more satisfaction to bury two families than to select and equip a home for one,"* he was not talking about this great house in Hartford. He and his family lived here from 1874 to 1891.

Goth Cottage

Designated as a National Historic Landmark in 1992, Roseland Cottage in Woodstock remains one of the nation's best preserved examples of Gothic Revival architecture, with its steep gables, decorative bargeboards, and ornamented chimney pots. The interior of Roseland Cottage provides visitors with a glimpse of the lifestyle and tastes of a Victorian family.

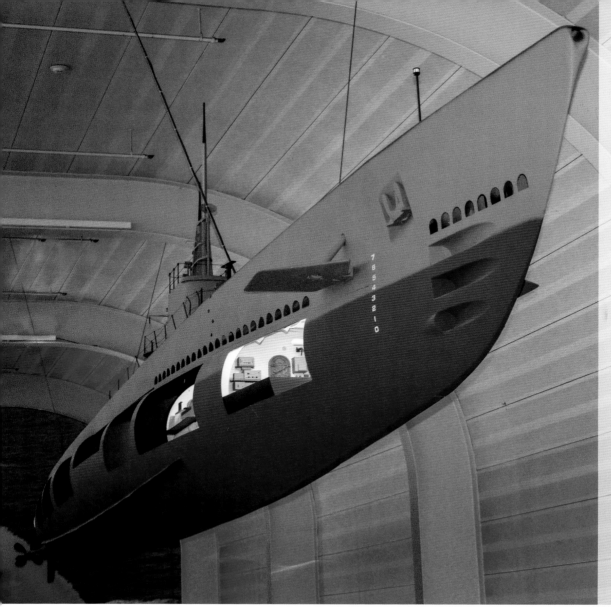

Suspended Submersible

One of the most impressive exhibits, and there are many, at the Submarine Force Museum located on the Thames River in Groton, Connecticut, is this 1/6th scale Gato class boat suspended from a Pacific Blue-colored ceiling. The museum is operated by the United States Navy and is considered to be the world's finest collection of submarine artifacts.

The Odd Couple
(opposite page)

A bright red tugboat gently shepherds this sinister US Navy attack submarine towards it's dock at Groton, CT. With some of the crew topside, the sub is returning to port after a mission. A crew members casts a mooring line to attendant vessels as friends and families of the crewmembers wait with anticipation on the pier.

Sabre to the Fore
(above)

This North American F-86F "Sabre" is only one of the fascinating exhibits at The New England Air Museum in Windsor Locks.

Three hangars and more than 75,000 square feet of exhibit space display more than 80 aircraft. Also featured are flight simulators, collections of engines, instruments, aircraft parts, uniforms and personal memorabilia.

Batterson's Revenge

The contract to build Hartford's State Capitol building was awarded to Richard M. Upjohn. The unsuccessful bidder, James G. Batterson, was retained as the building contractor. During construction, Batterson constantly revised Upjohn's plans to more resemble his own. This central tower is Batterson's design.

The Three Pioneers

The north face of the Capitol Building has six statues representing pre-Revolutionary War figures.

These, and other statues in and around the building, honor people who figure prominently in the history of Connecticut. Immortalized here are former governors John Winthrop the Younger, Theophilus Eaton, and traveler, amateur artist, architect and arts patron, Daniel Wadsworth.

Evelyn's Victory

The Spanish-American War Memorial in Bushnell Park features the statue, *Spirit of Victory,* in the form of the Greek War goddess, Nike, by Evelyn Beatrice Longman. Evelyn was the first woman sculptor to be elected a full member of the National Academy of Design in 1919.

A Peaceful Oasis in the City

Bushnell Park, in Hartford was named for the Reverend Horace Bushnell, who officially proposed its creation to the City Council in 1853. It was not until 1861 that Swiss-born landscape architect Jacob Weidenmann, working with Bushnell, came up with a suitable design. As part of his plan, Weidenmann selected 157 varieties of deciduous and evergreen trees and shrubs from all over the world for inclusion in the park.

MASSACHUSETTS

Province Lands, Cape Cod National Seashore

Hard to Miss
The History

With 57 listings of National Historic Properties in a city known for it's suitability for walking, it is difficult to find any area of Boston without something historically interesting! Shown here, within a short distance of each other, are the USS *Constitution*, Faneuil Hall and a statue of Founding Father Samuel Adams.

Pastries, Eggs and Inspiration

Merchants at the Copley Square Farmers Market offer their wares in front of Trinity Church.

Designed by Harry Hobson Richardson and consecrated on February 9, 1877, the granite and sandstone church soon thereafter had its facade and towers remodeled to resemble Richardson's own sketches of Romanesque Churches in Arles, France.

Dr. Warren's Obelisk

(opposite page)

The original monument on Breed's Hill was an 18-foot wooden pillar erected by Masons in 1794 to honor fallen patriot and mason, Dr. Joseph Warren. This 221-foot obelisk, now known as the Bunker Hill monument, was built of granite quarried in Quincy, MA, and completed in 1842. The exhibit lodge houses a statue of Dr. Warren.

Root Vegetables and Italian Architecture

On Tuesdays and Fridays, Copley Square is transformed into a colorful Farmer's Market where office workers can pick up top quality fresh produce for home meals, or for a quick lunch. In the background are the Northern Italian Gothic styled Campanile and Lantern of the "New" Old South Church.

The Big House in The Cow Pasture

Built in 1798, the "new" State House is located on the top of Beacon Hill; land originally used as John Hancock's cow pasture.

The original wooden dome was overlaid with copper by Paul Revere. In 1874, 23-karat gold leaf was applied. It was painted black during World War II to confuse anticipated bombing raids.

Hancock, Hancock and Beacon

Reflected in the younger (1976) John Hancock Tower is the 1947 Old John Hancock Tower. This art deco building provides Bostonians with quick weather predictions. The lights in the spire are blue for blue skies, flashing blue for cloudy, red when it is going to rain, and flashing red when snow is forecast.

Wicked Good on a Bun!

Try not to eat before you visit Quincy Market; for there you will discover a huge food court where you can sample cuisines from all over the world. Lobster, clam chowder, pasta, stir fry, sushi, bagels, and pizza compete for the appetite along with this fine selection of Boston sausage.

Old Church —Older Neighborhood

The Old North Church, built in 1723, is the oldest standing church building in Boston.

Visitors to the church are well-advised to wander through the cobblestone streets of the surrounding North End. Authentic Italian restaurants, cafes and pastry shops flourish in the city's oldest residential community, which was first settled in the 1630s.

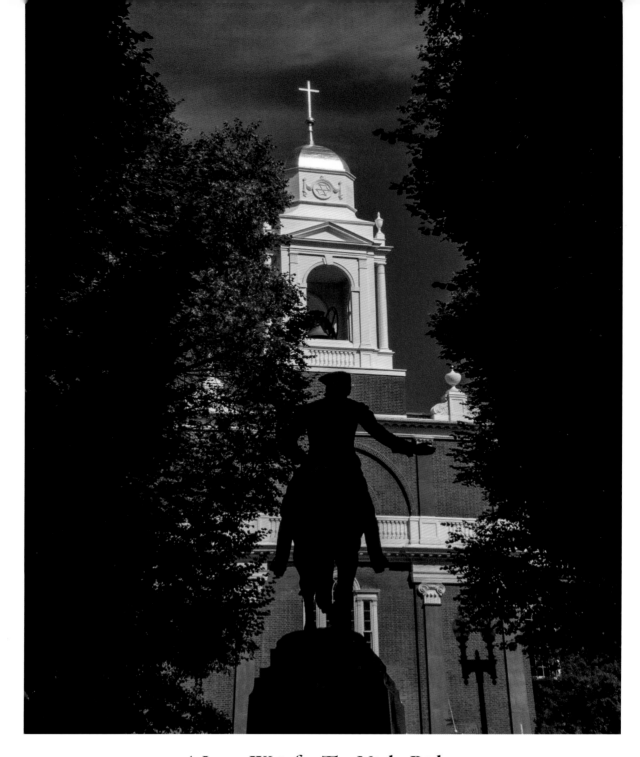

A Long Wait for The Night Rider

The statue of Paul Revere, near St. Stephen's Church, is one of the most recognized landmarks in Boston. Finally completed in 1899, after over 16 years of design revisions, the statue then languished for another 40 years before being placed in this pleasant tree-lined park with a fountain and brick paving.

Chatham's Golden Sands

Below the US Coast Guard station at Chatham is the is the ever-changing landscape of Lighthouse Beach, the largest in town.

Located a short walk from downtown, this beautiful expanse of sand offers nature walks out to southern Monomoy Island plus views of the daily migration routes of Chatham's many seals and passing fishing boats.

Cape Cod Wines

Truro Vineyards has been in existence since 1992, but the house and the estate date back nearly two centuries. The 1813 Federal farmhouse was the subject of a 1930 painting by the famous American artist Edward Hopper. Once a producer of cantaloupes, the warm, well-drained soil has proved to be a perfect spot for growing grapes.

Walk Towards the Light

The Wood End Light, near Provincetown is a 38-foot brick tower that was placed into service on November 20, 1872.

The lighthouse was automated in 1961 and converted to solar power in 1981.

The light can be reached by a brisk 30-minute walk across the breakwater, which was built in 1911.

Plymouth Only Has a Rock

(opposite page)

The Pilgrim Monument, completed in 1910, commemorates the first landing of the Mayflower Pilgrims in Provincetown on November 21, 1620.

Built with granite from Stonington, Maine, and measuring over 252 feet tall, the monument qualifies as the tallest all-granite structure in the US.

The design is patterned after the Torre del Mangia in Siena, Spain.

Beacon Vanquishes Ghost

Eighteenth Century Cape Cod mariners told of a ghostly rider on a white horse, who appeared on stormy nights on the treacherous waters off Chatham, swinging a lantern that lured mariners to their doom.

A light station was established in 1808. This tower, now part of a USCG Station, was built in 1877 and automated in 1982.

A Real Yankee Swap

The Meetinghouse was the universally recognized symbol of the New England town in the early 19th century. This building, which now serves Sturbridge Village, was obtained from the local Baptist Society, which agreed to exchange the structure for an organ for their new church. The building was taken apart, moved, and reassembled as a museum exhibit.

That Old Saw

(opposite page)

After thoroughly researching the original site of David Wight's (1761–1813) long-extinct sawmill, then examining historical documentation and conducting extensive research, Sturbridge Village staff built this replica of a period up-and-down saw and placed it upon the same spot.

It is now a working mill that produces sawn boards for use in the museum.

A Sturbridge Stroll

Old Sturbridge Village allows the visitor to experience early New England life from 1790–1840. One of the country's largest living history museums, the village features authentically costumed staff, called history interpreters, carrying out the daily activities of an early 19th-century community. The Village, now covering over 200 acres, features antique buildings, water-powered mills and a working farm.

Made by Hand — Just Add Water

This hand-built wooden boat awaits final finishing in this busy boatyard in Vineyard Haven.

The boat is a Nat Benjamin designed, 11-foot sailing tender, built using lapstrake construction methods.

Nat Benjamin and his business partner, Ross Gammon, have built over 50 vessels at this location near the ocean on Martha's Vineyard.

Once a Guardian, Now a Memorial

In 1939, the old Edgartown lighthouse was replaced with an 1881 vintage cast-iron tower relocated from Ipswich, MA. Now in private hands, it has been modernized and solar powered. It is now the site of the Children's Memorial, where children's names, carved into granite cobblestones are placed permanently into the foundation of the lighthouse.

Baker and Fudge Maker

Life imitates art as a Murdick's fudge maker prepares to slice a loaf into 8 ounce portions. Murdick's Fudge was established in 1887 on Mackinac Island in Michigan. The first of three stores on Martha's Vineyard was established in Edgartown, in this building which previously housed the Post Office.

From Orphaned Puppy to Vineyard Icon

When Captain Douglas, the founder of the Black Dog Tavern and General Store, adopted a black puppy and named him after the pirate character in the classic book *Treasure Island,* he probably had no idea that the image of the dog would become representative of all that was Martha's Vineyard.

The Black Dog General Stores, Bakeries and Tavern are popular tourist destinations throughout New England.

Fabulous Water Views
From Every Seat

Situated right next to the small drawbridge that crosses the gap between the Great Harbor and Eel Pond, the Fishmonger, a casual café in Woods Hole offers patrons fresh seafood and wholesome meals. Diners may observe boats that come and go from Eel Pond, and enjoy the view of Vineyard Sound.

Addressing
the Peasants

This British Officer reenactor makes comments, with an authentic attitude of disdain, to the spectators at the Bloody Angle Battle Site in Lincoln, MA. Each year, in mid-April, thousands of people flock to historic Lexington, Concord and Minute Man National Historical Park to celebrate Patriot's Day and witness parades, Revolutionary War reenactments and commemorative ceremonies.

Friendship With a Storehouse

The original Salem East Indiaman *Friendship,* launched in 1797, served as a merchant vessel. She completed 15 voyages before being captured by the British in 1812. This replica of *Friendship* was built using modern materials, but retains the appearance of the original ship.

The 1770 Pedrick Store House was acquired from the town of Marblehead.

Nathaniel Hawthorne's Office?
—First Floor, Left

Hawthorne worked here as a surveyor from 1836–1839. The author prefaced his 1850 novel *The Scarlet Letter* with a virtual tour of this building. Built in 1819, and the last in a succession of 13 Salem customs houses, this building now displays and exhibits of the history of the US Customs Service, and Nathaniel Hawthorne's office.

Ahoy, Below!

(above)

These young visitors peer into the darkened lower decks of the *Mayflower II,* a replica of the 17th century ship which transported the Pilgrims to the New World.

Built in Devon, England, during 1955 and 1956, this ship then recreated the original 55-day voyage, sailing across the Atlantic Ocean to Plymouth.

Welcome to the 17th Century

(opposite page)

The English Village, the largest open-air section of the Plimoth Plantation, approximates the layout of the original settlement that was established in the 17th century by English colonists, who are now commonly referred to as Pilgrims. The museum, started in 1947, accurately depicts the lives of the Wampanoag communities and Plymouth colonists.

Forging a Career
(*above*)

Amodern-day advertisement for the position of Apprentice to the Blacksmith at Plimoth Plantation, where interpreters portray life in the year 1627, requires that the applicant must: *"perform strenuous manual labor on a regular basis, including; striking for the Blacksmith with an eight-pound sledgehammer and lifting and moving objects in excess of one hundred pounds."*

An Elk. Presented by the Elks

In 1923, on land donated by Charles H. Canedy, the owner of the nearby Whitcomb Summit, this magnificent monument was placed to honor members of the Greenfield Elk Club who died in World War I.

The Elk was built by the Gorham Manufacturing Co. The $6,000 cost was mainly raised by Massachusetts Elk organizations.

Flowers in The Rain

The Bridge of Flowers is a major attraction, rain or shine. The bridge, built in 1908 for the Shelburne Falls and Colrain Street Railway, was redundant by 1928. The Shelburne Woman's Club transformed the bridge into a garden. In 1983, the bridge was restored. During the restoration, every plant removed was cared for in private.

Tanglewood's Victorian Visitor Center

Tanglewood Music Center in Lenox, Massachusetts, has been the summer home of the Boston Symphony Orchestra since 1934. The property, which covers over 200 acres, features the famous Koussevitzky Music Shed with the surrounding great lawn seating thousands; the modern Seiji Ozawa Hall; beautiful landscaping; spectacular views of the Berkshires and many historic homes.

Beethoven's Casual Day

On summer weekends, the Tanglewood Music Shed and the adjoining lawn are a popular destination for many summer visitors who, equipped with lawn chairs, blankets, food and beverages, are treated to a full Open Rehearsal by the Boston Symphony Orchestra of works to be presented later in the weekend.

The Misty
River Flows

(opposite page)

New England is justifiably famous for it's fall colors. Although there are many established "leaf-peeper" routes, glorious examples of color can be found in many unexpected places. On this quiet back road near the town of Ipswich, a ghostly low lying mist flows silently across a country road.

Still Watchful
After All These Years

(above)

Inspired by a 1901 painting by Augustus Buhler, the 8-foot-tall bronze Fishermen's Memorial, also known as *The Man At The Wheel,* was unveiled in 1925. The sculptor, Leonard Craske, spent many hours aboard fishing vessels, watching the fishermen work.

Captain Clayton Morrissey, a prominent Gloucester fisherman, posed for the statue.

By the Dawn's
Early Light

The fishing fleet remains at dock in Gloucester as, although the boats are lit up by the brilliant gold light of the rising sun, the dark clouds above, and to seaward indicate a day best spent safe.

Rockport's Famous Red House

Referred to as Motif Number 1, the fishing shack located on Bradley Wharf is well known to students of art and art history as *"the most often-painted building in America."* The town, recognizing its iconic value, has taken pains to preserve both its structure and appearance, finding a red paint which appears weather-beaten even when new.

Like a Childhood Dream

A classic schooner passes the Hammond Castle in Magnolia.

Prolific inventor John Hays Hammond, Jr. built his medieval-style castle between the years 1926 and 1929. Visitors to the Hammond Castle Museum may explore the castle on self-guided tours and enjoy special events held there; one of the most popular being Halloween.

MAINE

Bar Harbor

A Casual Fleet Review

The coastline of Acadia National Park is constantly being reformed by the action of the waves and currents of the Atlantic Ocean. Sand eroded from the rocks is deposited here at Sand Beach, a small and cozy beach tucked between two rocky headlands.

Sharp and Smooth Granite
(opposite page)

Otter Cliffs is the most popular rock climbing destination in Acadia National Park. Rugged granite cliffs rise up to 110 feet directly from the ocean; contrasting sharply with an adjacent beach of smooth round boulders. The cliff is so popular with climbers that there are permanent climbing rope anchors at the top.

Awed by the Beauty of Acadia

Established as a national site in 1916, the 49,000-acre park is a favorite destination for visitors from all over the world, who come to hike over granite peaks, bike on historic carriage roads and enjoy the spectacular scenery.

Two Views of
The First Sunrise

(right and below)

The summit of Cadillac Mountain; to witness "the nation's first sunrise," is a popular destination for visitors to Acadia National Park. One of many photographers, eager to capture the event, is oblivious to the full moon; while another visitor snuggles down in a sweatshirt for a more individual viewing experience.

A Lighthouse
in it's Element

(opposite page)

The red fresnel lens, manufactured in Paris in 1901, in the Bass Harbor Head Lighthouse warns mariners of danger in the mist at the entrance to Bass Harbor, on the southwestern side of Mount Desert Island. The lighthouse, built in 1858 of brick on a stone foundation, stands 56 feet above mean high water.

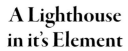

Don't Tread on this Carpet of Red

Gaylussacia baccata— commonly known as huckleberry, is a low-growing, deciduous shrub that changes color to dramatic red in the fall. Although the plant is hardy, the stems and twigs are quite delicate. The berries produced provide food for many mammals and birds of Acadia.

Sparkling Water From Maine
(opposite page)

There are many substantial rivers in Maine, but don't overlook the little streams in the woods for a delightful image. This mini-cascade dances over granite rocks strewn with the colors of fall as it makes it's way towards the Atlantic Ocean.

Nature's Contrast

Light feathery ferns, a species of Rock Polypody, grow on top of this large granite boulder in Acadia National Park. The cool, moist climate of coastal Maine provides an ideal climate for unique displays of plant life.

Acadia Skies
(left)

Visitors to the Jordan Pond House restaurant may indulge in the long-standing tradition of having afternoon tea on the lawn while enjoying the spectacular view of "the Bubbles."

(below)

Wildflowers on a cliff top reach toward a bright blue sky. A recent survey documented over 860 species of wildflowers, ferns, grasses, sedges, rushes, trees, and shrubs.

Mainly Maine Art
(opposite page, below, left)

With a permanent collection entitled *Maine in America,* the Farnsworth Museum in Rockland emphasizes the role of Maine artists in American Art. Great American painters and sculptors such as Gilbert Stuart, Thomas Sully, Futz Hugh Lane and Louise Neveson are also well represented. Exhibits are also housed at the Wyeth Center, Farnsworth Homestead and the Olson House.

The Big Bean Boot

L.L.Bean was founded by Leon Leonwood Bean in 1912. With the opening of the store, Mr. Bean threw the keys of the shop in Greenwood Lake, saying: *"We don't need the keys. We will never close."* This location in Freeport, originally opened in 1917, has been open 24 hours a day since 1951.

Supplies for Frye
(above)

*T*he ferry from Raymond Neck heads for Frye Island in Sebago Lake. Contractors are busy in the summer, maintaining the vacation homes of the seasonal residents. Frye Island is vacant from November through April, as the ferry does not operate during that time, due to the formation of thick ice on the lake.

A Slice of Portland History

This wedge-shaped building in Portland Square is known as the "upper" H. H. Hay Building. There is a "lower" Hay building within a few blocks.

Built in 1826, it was originally occupied by H.H. Hay, a chemist commended by his peers in the *"Druggist's Circular and Chemical Gazette,"* for publishing, in 1902, a tourist (and advertising) brochure called *"Summer Trips Around Portland, Maine."*

Mullet's Second Empire

After the destruction of several federal properties in fires, Supervising Architect of the Treasury, Alfred Bult Mullett, decreed that "fireproof" federal buildings should be located on single lots in order to provide better protection from fire jumping. Mullett chose the "Second Empire" architectural style, usually reserved for huge federal buildings, for the design of this Portland customhouse. Construction was completed in 1872.

Forget the Fish! Come on Out and Throw the Ball!

This dog is only interested in the return of his master, who is visiting the famous Harbor Fish Market located on the historic Portland waterfront. The picturesque, historic storefront has served as a backdrop for numerous print and television advertisements, paintings, photographs, and post cards.

Where the Red Paint Ran Out

This the seaward side of the Harbor Fish Market; known for it's famous bright red façade; where boats can unload their catch right at the back door. A family owned and operated business for over 40 years, this quaint location is well known for selling top quality fish and seafood.

Talk and Cut Bait

(above)

A cheerful conversation is carried on by this Rockport lobsterman and his friend in the early hours of a summer's day. After preparing fresh baits dockside, the fisherman will head out to haul the traps from the previous set, (hopefully all containing legal size lobsters) and then rebait and reset them.

On Her Way to Work
(opposite page)

*W*ith the Owl's Head Light in the background, the Rockport fishing boat *Brenda Lee* heads out to check a trap set. Although the fishing is hard work, there are respites during the season with numerous Lobster Festivals and Lobster Boat races in several different picturesque ports.

Bridge With Flowers
(above)

*W*hen the entrance to a picturesque coastal town includes a flower-lined bridge, you know it is a special place. Rockport is known for being a cultural and artistic town; with it's own large community of local artists; and as a destination for artists from all over the world.

Different Boats
for Different Folks
(above)

In a scene often repeated in the numerous small harbors of coastal Maine, different types of craft; from sleek restored antique sailboats with varnished wood and hand-lettered custom paint, to work-scarred and purposeful-looking fishing boats share the moorings and ride the tides.

Pleasant Light
on Pleasure Craft
(opposite page)

Arranged around a small village of a dozen historic buildings, the delightful Penobscot Marine Museum in Searsport is designed to entertain and educate visitors of all ages to the tastes, talents and challenges of maritime life.

This old carriage house is home to *Rowboats and Rusticators,* an exhibit of historic Maine recreational boats.

Picture Framer, Framed

*T*he owner of the Tidemark Gallery in Waldoboro prepares a painting for hanging with the works of other artists in this charming gallery. The gallery was founded in 2006 to help show the work of local artists, many of whom interpret views of the Medomak River, rolling hills, and historic farmhouses, buildings and homes.

The Chocolate Church
(right)

*T*he Central Congregational Church in Bath is an impressive Gothic Revival structure, raised in 1847. In the late 1970s, the church was painted a dark brown color and became known as the "Chocolate Church." In 1981, the interior was reconfigured as a performing arts center, and took on a new role to present music, theater and visual arts.

Federal Style and Hot Pink Chairs

*T*he Reed Mansion, in Waldoboro, is also known as "Cuttings Folly."

Rev. John Cutting started building this house in 1809, but lacking the funds to complete it, sold it to Col. Isaac Reed in 1812. Reed was instrumental in both the drafting of the constitution of Maine, and the design of the State seal.

Sundays at Tiffany's
(left)

*A*s part of the 1902 renovations of the First Congregational Church in Searsport new memorial stained-glass windows were installed. It is commonly believed that the windows were created by the now famous Tiffany Studios.

Vertical Variety

(right, and below)

There's a lot of tall things in Camden, Maine. From church steeples and weathervanes, to the masts of a windjammer. Luckily, only some have to be climbed. One of the most scenic harbors in Maine, and a departure point for many windjammers, the picturesque village also offers a selection of shops and galleries to satisfy every need.

Night Watch

(opposite page)

With oil lamps still burning, the schooner *Timberwind* greets a dawn in Rockport. Since her launching in Portland in 1931, she has never left Maine waters. Originally the Portland Pilot Boat, she has been extensively restored to provide comfortable

accommodations for short or long-term seafaring adventures in the cruising grounds of Penobscot Bay.

Fishing the Offshore Island

A fisherman tries his luck in the narrow channel between the Continental United States and the "Nubble."

The "Nubble" is a small, rocky island a short distance off the eastern point of Cape Neddick, about two miles north of York Harbor.

Deserving of it's Title
(right, and opposite page)

*T*hese two images, taken within an hour of each other, show why the Portland Head Light on Cape Elizabeth is described by locals as *"the most photographed lighthouse in the world."*

It was commissioned by George Washington and dedicated by the Marquis de Lafayette upon completion in 1791.

Carlton at Dawn

*T*he Carlton Bridge in Bath was opened in 1927 and carried rail, automobile and pedestrian traffic until the year 2000, when the nearby Sagadahoc bridge was opened. The 3,093 ft long bridge still carries the traffic of the Maine Eastern Railroad.

Giants in the Mist
(right)

*H*uge dockside cranes loom above this destroyer under construction at the Bath Iron Works. Commissioned as the USS *Michael Murphy* in October, 2012, this ship is named in honor of Medal of Honor winner Michael Patrick Murphy; the first MOH recipient for actions in Afghanistan; and the first for the U.S. Navy since the Vietnam War.

Sailor's Delight
(opposite page)

*W*ith enough wind to gladden the heart of any sailor, this Maine schooner races across West Penobscot Bay. Schooner cruises, available at several locations on the coast of Maine, range in length from a few hours to several days. Specialty cruises include programs for those interested in nature watching, photography, gourmet food and wine, festivals and fireworks.

NEW HAMPSHIRE

The Mount Washington Hotel

The Lieutenant Colonel's Lighthouse

(above)

This 48 ft tall Portsmouth, NH lighthouse, built in 1878, is a fine example of the low-maintenance, brick-lined, cast iron design developed by the Lighthouse Board. The design was penned by US Army Engineer officer James C. Duane, a decorated Civil War veteran. It was assembled inside the previous, larger tower, which was then removed.

Cats are Allowed on This Beach

(opposite page, top)

The "Catamaran Regatta" has become a highlight of the summer at Hampton Beach as experienced and novice sailors converge for a weekend of competitive sailing. The weekend is well organized with several races throughout the day, all held close to the shore so that visitors and non-sailors can admire the spectacle.

Oranges in the Strawbery

(right)

*C*hase House is one of the grandest Georgian structures at "Strawbery Banke," an outdoor history museum featuring more than 40 restored buildings built between the 17th and 19th centuries. The museum is located in the South End historic district of Portsmouth.

German Street Art in Portsmouth

This mural by the talented German duo Herakut (she's Hera, he's Akut) brightens this wall of a store on State Street. The Portsmouth Museum of Art commissioned renowned artists from Germany, Greece and California to produce artworks for their *Street a.k.a. Museum* exhibit.

Artist's Delight

Framed by the sculpture *Beauty: The Common Denominator* by Walter Liff, the 59-foot tall Whaleback Light stands on the northeast side of Portsmouth Harbor. Since 1820, there have been several variants of the light. The current structure, dating from 1872, is based on the famous Eddystone Light in the UK. The ferry boat is the M/V *Thomas Laighton*.

Neptune in Prescott Park

Prescott Park occupies over 10 acres of waterfront along the Piscataqua River. This fountain, a statue of Neptune, is a memorial to Ensign Charles Emerson Hovey of the US Navy, who was killed in action in the Philippines in 1911. The statue was given to the city by his mother, Mrs. Louise Folsom Hovey.

A Special Lake: Sunapee

Before the advent of the automobile, visitors to Lake Sunapee experienced a train ride to lakeside depots like Sunapee Harbor. There, they boarded steamers that ferried them to the numerous lakeside grand hotels and resort lodges, where, surrounded by majestic mountains, they fished, swam and sailed upon sparkling clear waters.

Ginger's Lake Light

*T*here are 5 lighthouses in New Hampshire. As the state has only 18 miles of coastline, it is not surprising to find 3 of them on Sunapee Lake.

Herrick Cove Light was built in 1893 and restored in 2003, in part with funds raised in memory of the daughter of George Cross, chair of the Lake Sunapee Protective Association. The light is also known as Ginger's Light.

Determined to Stay in Stark

This covered bridge, constructed in 1862, crosses the Ammonoosuc River at Stark, NH.

In the late 1800s, the bridge was carried down the river by a flood. It was dragged back into place using oxen. A 1950s attempt to replace the bridge with a new structure was defeated by artists and covered bridge enthusiasts.

The Chapel With the Paper Windows

Dedicated in 1894, St. Matthews had modest beginnings. Seated upon wooden benches, the congregation viewed a "window" behind the altar that was made of paper, painted to resemble stained glass.

Fine stained glass windows, three from a church in NY, and one from Tiffany, now grace this lovely church in Sugar Hill.

No Rest on the Sabbath

Sabbaday Falls is a 3-tier waterfall just off the Kancamagus Highway in Waterville. The upper fall drops about 8 feet into a deep emerald punchbowl, spills over a 20 foot horsetail, then makes a sharp right turn and flows through a deep flume to a crystal-clear pool.

Just Follow This River to the Wilderness

The Lincoln Woods Trail, in the White Mountain National Forest, follows this East branch of the Pemigewasset River and leads into one of the largest roadless areas in the Eastern United States, the Pemigewasset Wilderness. The Lincoln Woods Trailhead, on the Kancamagus Highway, is just to the right of this image.

Quiet Please! There May be Fairies About!

Approximately 10,000 years ago, large volumes of water carrying sand, gravel and boulders from melting glaciers carved out the Sabbaday Falls gorge. After the boisterous journey over the falls, the Sabbaday Brook flows quietly into this enchanting grotto. Wooden steps, bridges and handrails line a short walk from the parking lot to ensure easy access to this natural wonder.

Natural Chat Room

Although many visitors to Lake Winnipesaukee engage in active pursuits such as water skiing, tubing, snorkeling, scuba diving and swimming, the lake is big enough to have quiet sheltered corners such as this at Weir's Beach. An ideal location to relax in the gentle waves and catch up on conversation with a friend.

A Big Boat in the Pool
(left)

Bathers at Lake Winnipesaukee seem completely indifferent to the passage of the MS *Mount Washington*.

A conversion from a Lake Champlain side-wheeler, she was launched in 1940. Several modifications have been made to the ship since then and she now sails round-trips on the lake by day, and offers dinner and dance cruises in the evenings.

Haggis in New Hampshire

*T*he NH Highland Games, held annually at Loon Mountain, features athletic and music competitions, sheep dog trials, massed bands and authentic Celtic music, foods and products.

Viaduct to Nowhere

At the end of a small road just off Highway 93 near Echo Lake, there are two surprises. A monument to Governor Hugh J. Gallen, and this graceful 312-foot long bridge, which spans the Lafayette Creek.

Formerly part of the highway, it now carries only bikers and hikers as part of the Franconia Notch Recreation Path.

Symmetry of Green Ski Runs

Cannon Mountain Ski Area, in Franconia Notch State Park, features 9 ski lifts and the only aerial tram in New Hampshire to get up the mountain; and 22 miles of trails, including the most vertical runs in NH, to get back down. US Olympic skier Bode Miller honed his skills here.

Spanish Renaissance Style—by Italian Craftsmen

Industrialist Joseph Stickney spent 1.7 million dollars in to create the luxurious Mount Washington Hotel in New Hampshire's White Mountains. Two hundred fifty Italian artisans were imported to build the granite and stucco masonry. Opened in 1902, this magnificent 200-room hotel offers numerous resort activities including fishing, hiking, horseback riding, sleigh rides and more.

Sylvester's Little Steam Engines

The Mount Washington Cog Railway came into being because inventor Sylvester Marsh got lost in a storm on Mt Washington and wanted an easier way down.

The first ascent of the 3.1 mile track to the summit was completed in 1869. Since then, tilt-boiler locomotives have carried thousands of visitors on this special ride.

Don't Forget to Look Up

From a walkway above a rushing stream in the Flume Gorge it is easy to become entranced by the sights below. A glance upwards reveals an equally fascinating sight; moss-covered granite walls rising 80 feet to equally tall trees and the sky.

Aunt Guernsey's Gorge
(opposite page)

The Flume is an 800-foot long natural gorge on the Pemigewasset River near Lincoln. The walls of granite rise to an average height of 80 feet and are 12 to 20 feet apart. This natural phenomenon was discovered in 1808 by 93-year-old "Aunt" Jess Guernsey, when she accidentally came upon it while fishing.

Destruction and Creation

Initially, a 10 ft by 12 ft boulder was suspended between the walls of the Flume Gorge. In June of 1883, a heavy rainstorm started a landslide that swept the boulder from its place. It has never been found. The same storm formed these Avalanche Falls, and deepened the gorge to it's present depth.

This View Will be Forever

Recognizing that the shore lands of lakes like this one in Lincoln are among its most valuable and fragile natural resources, the Shoreland Water Quality Protection Act, enacted into law in 1991, establishes a "Protected Shoreland" area along New Hampshire's lakes, rivers and coastline, and regulates construction and land use within those areas.

Little River Jumps Off a Cliff

Glen Ellis Falls, a short walk from Route 16 near Pinkham Notch, is well worth a visit. It is unusual, in that it is first viewed from the top, where a sparkling little river chortles along, then, after making a sharp left turn, leaps 60 feet to the rocks below.

Water at Work in Littleton

The red building is the Littleton Grist Mill, dating from 19th century. The Ammonoosuc River turns the overshot wheel, which uses 24-inch stones to grind grain into authentic "stone ground" flour. A modern electric mill produces waffle and pancake mixes and flours, which are sold in specialty shops throughout the Northeast.

The Honeymoon Bridge

The Jackson covered bridge was built in 1876 by Charles and Frank Broughton. The bridge is known locally as the "Honeymoon Bridge," based on the tradition of young couples using the shaded passages to steal a kiss. The custom has carried on with many newly-married couples having their picture taken at the bridge.

A Change in Eagle Attitude

(above)

The New Hampshire State House, completed in 1819, is the oldest State House in the nation in which the legislature still occupies its original chambers.

In 1818, a statue of a huge, gold-painted wooden war eagle was raised on the dome. In 1957, it was replaced with a weather-proof peace eagle statue.

Ready for Halloween

(opposite page, below)

The predominant color in New Hampshire's fall is gold, and these pumpkins have attained that hue, which indicates that they are ready for either carving into jack-o-lanterns or baking into pies. At this time of year, farm stands also feature corn mazes, hay rides and great local-made products: cheese, maple syrup, honey, eggs, pies, jams and breads.

"Admired by Every Looker Over"
(above)

B uilt with cash subscriptions and donations of labor of the congregation, (although there was an architect's bill of $2.00) this "Little White Church" (as it is now known) in Eaton was described upon completion in 1879, as *"a good structure, well build and of good proportion and admired by nearly every looker over."* (sic)

RHODE ISLAND

Fort Adams State Park

All Eyes on The Lines

(above)

A fisherman examines the tension on his line as the crew of a sailboat in the background concentrate on the set of their sails, in this image which illustrates different nautical pastimes in Newport. The harbor enjoys a rich diversity of activities such as fishing, sailing, antique boat rendezvous, regattas, races and recreational boating.

Arabella at the Bridge

(opposite page, above)

Considered by many to be the sailing capital of the world, Newport is still home to many former America's Cup entrants and other classic sailing craft. The ideal sailing conditions around the harbor and Narragansett Bay also provide a playground for charter boats such as this 155 foot tri-masted staysail schooner *Arabella,* seen here against the backdrop of the Newport Bridge.

Planning a Boisterous Celebration? Rent a Fort!

(right)

Fort Adams, the home of generations of soldiers from 1824 to 1950 is now the site of public music festivals (including the famous Newport Jazz and Folk Festivals) fireworks displays, summer ghost hunts and many other events. The site is also available for private parties and weddings.

Waterfront Mansion.
With Lobster Boat.

Newport is home to some of the most sumptuous mansions in the US. Although many are gathered in Newport itself, some are positioned with a view of the Atlantic Ocean. Sharing these locations are the working fishing boats of Rhode Island's lobstermen.

Boutiques, Antiques, and Cobblestone Streets

*I*f you have some time left after enjoying Newport's numerous festivals, or touring opulent ocean-side mansions, interesting museums, and historic coastal forts, lighthouses, and worship buildings, take a stroll through the historic waterfront shopping district.

This lively area is home to art galleries, antique shops, boutiques, sailing shops and much more.

"Would You Like 'em Cooked, or Kickin,' Sir?"

*T*he Newport Lobster Shack, operated by the Fishermen of Newport Association, is located on Long Wharf and sells lobsters, crabs and conch fresh off the boat.

Up to 25 fishermen contribute their catch to the tanks daily, which can provide up to 1,200 pounds of fresh lobster for the public.

By Ferry to your Vacation Adventure

Rose Island Lighthouse, built in 1869, is located on an 18 acre island in Narragansett Bay. Restored by the Rose Island Lighthouse Foundation, it is now an adventure travel destination, reached only by boat, where visitors can spend a night as a guest, or a week as the working "lighthouse keeper."

From Sentinel to Staterooms

The Nantucket Lightship WLV-612, seen here at Newport, was the last of the Nantucket Lightships, which were known as the "Guardian Angels of the North Atlantic." Decommissioned in 1985, the ship passed into private hands in 2000 and, after extensive restoration and modernization, is now a five stateroom luxury yacht available for charter.

A *Minx* for the Boys

Nathanael Herreshoff designed the original full-keel 12-1/2, which he called the Buzzards Bay Boy's Boat, as a sail trainer that could handle the sometimes rough conditions of Massachusetts's Buzzards Bay. Betty Herreshoff, an avid sailor, taught her sons to sail in this boat, *Minx*, which was restored in the family workshops.

"Reasonable Accommodations"

Torch is a 1929 Fisher's Island 31 designed by Sidney Herreshoff. One reviewer wrote— *"the boats are beautiful to look at, contain reasonable accommodations, and are outstanding sailers."*

She is on display at the Herreshoff Museum in Bristol, RI. The Museum, bordering beautiful Narragansett Bay, is regarded as one of the nation's most important historic maritime collections.

Giraffe Crossing

Opened in 1872, Roger Williams Park Zoo is one of the oldest zoos in the US. It is an integral part of southern New England's history and heritage, bringing excitement and discovery of the natural world to generations of visitors.

Over half a million people visit the Zoo annually, making it one of Rhode Island's top tourist attractions.

Want to Talk Turkey?

*T*he Narragansett turkey descends from wild turkeys and the domestic turkeys brought to America by colonists in the 1600s.

The Coggeshall Farm Museum is a living historical farm set on 48 acres in Bristol, Rhode Island. The museum depicts agrarian life in 1799 through live interpretation, historic structures, and heirloom plants and animals.

A Working Colonial Farm

Prescott Farm depicts early American architecture and
landscape in a country setting. Master Gardeners
manage the kitchen and herb gardens

Workshops are offered at Prescott Farm during the summer
and fall each year. Past workshops have included stonewall
building, blacksmithing, open hearth cooking, a beehive
tour and tasting, and wind energy past and present.

Wind Power-Transmitted by Wood

A windmill converts the energy of the wind into rotational energy by means of vanes called sails. Uppermost in this image is the horizontal, or upper, wooden axis, which is attached to the vanes. With the help of cast iron-edged wooden gear wheels, this axis drives the vertical shaft called the grinding shaft.

How Cotton Changed a River

By the late 1700s, many communities were located on the Blackstone River near small, water-powered grist mills. Industrial development along the Blackstone changed dramatically after 1793, when Samuel Slater opened Slater Mill, the first cotton mill in the United States to use mechanical spinning machines. By 1800, Pawtucket supported 29 cotton mills and there was one dam nearly every mile of the Blackstone River and its tributaries.

"Hands On" History

A group of young visitors are supervised by Wilkinson Mill staff as they use original machinery to complete projects.

The Wilkinson Mill, opened in 1810, contains the machine tool shop used to service the Slater Mill.

An 8-ton water wheel transfers power from the Blackstone River to belt-driven lathes, drills, sanders and other machines.

The Cobblestones of Providence
(above)

Also known as "The Renaissance City," Providence has undergone an amazing transformation in recent years.

A thriving arts scene features concerts, sculptures, and the WaterFire performances every summer. Waterplace Park and Riverwalk, is a remarkable collection of cobblestone walkways, plazas, pedestrian bridges, gondolas and other features intertwined with the downtown rivers.

A Dome of Distinction
(opposite page)

The dome of the Rhode Island State House is the fourth-largest self-supporting marble dome in the world, after St. Peter's Basilica, the Taj Mahal and the Minnesota State Capitol.

The gold-covered statue on top of the dome is the "Independent Man," representing the independent spirit of Roger Williams, founder of Providence and Rhode Island.

Fresh Flowers in the Inner City

Providence has dramatically and successfully redeveloped its downtown during the past fifty years. Projects that uncovered the city's natural rivers, relocated a large section of railroad underground, and created Waterplace Park have transformed an urban wasteland into a pleasant panorama of parkland, river walkways, and a home for a thriving arts scene.

Sure Beats a Limo!

These newlyweds escape the reception crowds for a leisurely cruise in one of the "La Gondolas" of Providence. The authentically restored gondolas are 36 feet in length and about 5 feet across. They each weigh approximately 1,800 pounds, yet are powered by just one man, the gondolier, using a 14 foot oar.

Playing With Fire

One of the main attractions of Providence's fantastic Waterfire Festival is the singer, songwriter and fire dancer "Spogga Hash." Here Mr. Hash demonstrates his prowess at fire twirling on the bow of a moving boat.

The Darkened Theater

A hush falls over the crowd gathered at WaterPlace Park as 19 fires are ignited to add their light to that of the 50 torches and luminaria candle lanterns surrounding the basin. WaterFire events are held on a regular schedule, beginning at the end of May and continuing into October.

VERMONT

The Window Garden, Hildene

Lincoln Luxury

In 1905, Robert Todd Lincoln, the only child of
Abraham and Mary Todd Lincoln to survive to
adulthood, completed this Georgian Revival mansion in
1905. Sited on a 300 foot promontory overlooking the
Battenkill Valley near the scenic village of Manchester,
"Hildene" was home to Lincoln descendants until 1975,
longer than any other Lincoln residence.

Flowers in the Potter's Yard

Once the H.W. Myers and Son mill, this rustic 1900s building was transformed into an active craft pottery that today is one of southern Vermont's most popular destinations. Much of Bennington's history includes the potteries. Capt. John Norton, a Revolutionary war veteran, built the first kiln in Bennington in 1793.

Dinner Table Decorations?

Although Bennington Pottery is famous for its beautiful and functional dinnerware, tavernware and bakeware, there are more whimsical pieces on display in the fascinating historic buildings that make up these showrooms.

Norman Rockwell's Neighborhood

The Arlington Green Covered Bridge was built in 1852 and spans the Battenkill River on Vermont Route 313, near the former home of Norman Rockwell. The river is popular with fly fishermen and kayakers.

Roy Arnold's Mile-Long Circus Parade

The Arnold Circus Parade has nearly 4,000 figures; all built on a one-inch-to-one-foot scale. The 500 ft length of the procession of miniature clowns, acrobats, animals, and circus wagons would, if life-sized, translate to a parade over a mile long.

Not a Quiet Retirement

In 1871, this lighthouse was constructed on Colchester Reef in Lake Champlain. After being damaged several time by storms and ice during its 80-year tenure on the lake, it would be expected that the lighthouse would have a quiet time after being transported to Shelburne and restored.

In 1961 it was struck by lightning, which caused a small fire.

Relocated Treasures

Shelburne Museum, founded in 1947 by Electra Havemeyer Webb, is a museum of art and Americana located in Shelburne, VT. Over 150,000 works are exhibited in 39 exhibition buildings, 25 of which were relocated to the 45-acre grounds.

The 80-foot-diameter Round Barn was moved from East Passumpsic, Vermont, to the Museum in 1985–86.

"Locomotive of the Presidents"

Rail Locomotive No. 220, built in 1915 by the American Locomotive Company, got its nickname for its service hauling special trains carrying Calvin Coolidge, Herbert Hoover, Franklin D. Roosevelt, and Dwight D. Eisenhower.

It was donated to the Shelburne Museum in 1956.

Garden Steamer

The steamboat *Ticonderoga* was built in 1906 at the Shelburne Shipyard on nearby Lake Champlain. In 1954, the 892-ton, 200 foot long ship was moved overland to its final mooring amongst the gardens on the Shelburne Museum grounds.

Abandon Diets, All Ye Who Enter Here

This archway, framing the famous "Cowmobile," leads to the factory of Ben & Jerry's Ice Cream in Waterbury, VT.

This "oasis of ice cream euphoria" features factory tours, a gift shop and the "scoop shop," which features ice cream cakes, sundaes, shakes, cones and fresh fruit smoothies.

Big Teddy the Doorman

Founded in 1981, Vermont Teddy Bears is now the largest seller of teddy bears by mail order and Internet. The company handcrafts each of its teddy bears, and produces almost 500,000 teddy bears each year.

Sales of bears in this Shelburne store are treated like "adoptions," and there are numerous outfits available to personalize your bear.

Pints on Parade

This lineup of different-sized syrup jugs at Sugar and Spice in Mendon, VT, represents only one consideration for purchasing maple syrup. Maple syrup is divided into two major grades and 3 sub-grades depending upon color. The Vermont grading system differs from that of the U.S. in maintaining a higher standard of product density.

I'm not the Vermont Frog. So What?

Vermont is one of 20 states to have a designated state amphibian. The Northern Leopard Frog was designated by the Vermont Legislature in 1998. This North American Bullfrog in Manchester is unconcerned, as his breed is recognized as the representative of three states—Iowa, Missouri and Oklahoma.

Wild and Blue and Edible, Too

Common chicory *(Cichorium intybus)* is a perennial, herbaceous plant most commonly seen with bright blue flowers.

Familiar as a wild plant on Europe's roadsides, it has now become naturalized in North America. The leaves and flowers are used in salads, the cooked roots are eaten, or used as a seasoning, especially in coffee substitutes.

A Really Big Barn

The Shelburne "Farm Barn" was completed in 1890. As the hub and headquarters for the model agricultural estate, it housed administrative offices; blacksmith, paint and carpentry shops; farm machinery; wagons; stables for work mules and storage rooms for harvested crops. It's main section is five stories high and it's courtyard covers nearly 2 acres.

Billy Said What? You're Kidding Me!

These nanny goats seem to be having a conversation, perched on tree stumps at Shelburne Farm's children's farmyard. The "milk-a-goat" opportunity is a popular activity for adventurous children of all ages.

Scheduled activities, conducted by trained educators and volunteers, focus on caring for a variety of typical farm animals.

Hackney Horse Haven

W. Seward Webb's dream was to breed a Hackney horse for Vermont farmers that was strong enough for a plow; and elegant enough for a carriage. He built this 375 ft long Breeding Barn in 1891, which remained the largest open-span wooden structure in America until 1939. Because of the advent of the automobile, its life as a horse breeding center was short-lived.

A Traditional Inn

Originally the 19th-century country home of Dr. William Seward and Lila Vanderbilt Webb, the Inn at Shelburne Farms on the shores of Lake Champlain was restored in 1987, and retains it's historic character.

The Inn continues a tradition of the warmth, informal elegance and hospitality enjoyed by guests for more than a century.

Hercules and the Rock of Ages

I t is more than appropriate that the name chosen for a locomotive that hauled granite at the Rock of Ages Quarry in Graniteville, VT is "Hercules." This 0-6-2T Baldwin Locomotive is now retired from that task and rests near a large mound of granite tailings near an old quarry.

Greek Architecture in Vermont Green

The State House in Montpelier, VT is one of the nation's oldest and best preserved state capitols still in use. This Greek Revival building is Vermont's third, and was built in 1859 on the same site as the second. The front portico features a statue of the leader of the Green Mountain Boys, Ethan Allen.

This Soldier Found Fame, but no Fortune

Seth Warner, regarded as a fine soldier for his actions during the Revolutionary War, particularly at the Battle of Bennington, gained fame and promotion for his command of the Green Mountain Boys. However, he did not avail himself of the business opportunities available after the war and died virtually penniless, forcing his widow to appeal to Congress for charity.

Pay Attention, Class!

The Bennington Museum, originally founded in 1852 to commemorate the Battle of Bennington, has since acquired paintings and sculpture by Vermont artists, children's toys, maps, books, and military artifacts.

The Grandma Moses exhibit features this authentic 19th Century schoolroom.

Porcelain Poodle Parade

The Museum is well known as a center for the study of the ceramics produced in Bennington by the Norton Pottery and the United States Pottery Company during the Nineteenth Century. The scope, diversity and size of the museum's collections of Bennington pottery and porcelain is unequaled. These poodles were manufactured in the mid-1800s by the United States Pottery Co.

New England
... a fresh perspective